MONEY AND SOCIAL JUSTICE

By the

REV. F. H. DRINKWATER

I0145536

LONDON

BURNS OATES & WASHBOURNE LTD.

PUBLISHERS TO THE HOLY SEE

MADE AND PRINTED IN GREAT BRITAIN
FOR
BURNS OATES & WASHBOURNE LTD.
1934

PATER PAUPERUM
DATOR MUNERUM
LUMEN CORDIUM

CONTENTS

MONEY AND SOCIAL JUSTICE

QUADRAGESIMO ANNO AND HIGH FINANCE

A sermon preached in the Church of the Holy
Family, Birmingham, January, 1933.

' You cannot serve God and Mammon.'—
Matt. vi. 24.

IT is over a year ago now since our Holy Father
Pope Pius XI sent out to the Catholic world his
encyclical letter, called *Quadragesimo Anno*, on the
reconstruction of the social order. It is a long letter
of 70 pages in English. The first part of it recalls
and repeats the teaching of Pope Leo XIII forty
years ago in his letter, *Rerum Novarum*, about social
problems, and the last part sketches out the true
remedies of Catholic teaching in contrast with the
false remedies of Socialism and Communism. But in
the middle of his letter the Pope has a section describ-
ing the present-day situation as it has developed
since the days of Leo XIII ; and it is to this section
I want to draw your attention. The Holy Father's

words are of immense importance and urgency; the truth and the urgency of them is seen more clearly with every month that goes by.

As the Pope sees it, then, the social question to-day is no longer a question between employers and employed, as it was in the days of Leo XIII. Employers and employed, and unemployed, too, are now all in the same boat, all helpless in the power of high finance. These are his words :—

' It is obvious in our days that wealth and immense power have become concentrated in the hands of a few men. These few exercise in the economic sphere a domination that is despotic. It is not only their own money they can use; frequently as trustees and directors these few men control invested funds and administer them at their own good pleasure.

' This power becomes particularly irresistible when exercised by those who, because they hold and control money, are able also to govern credit and decide to whom it shall be allotted. In that way they supply the life-blood, so to speak, of the whole economic body. They have their grasp on the very soul of production, so that no one dare breathe against their will. . . . '

And again: ' The desire for profits has been followed by the unbridled ambition for domination. The whole economic side of life has become hard, cruel, and relentless to a ghastly extent.

' Furthermore, business affairs have become scandalously mixed up with the duties and offices of the civil authority ; this has led to crying evils, and has gone so far as to degrade the majesty of the State.

' The State ought to be the supreme arbiter. It should rule in kingly fashion far above all contention of parties. It should be intent only upon justice and public good. Instead, the State has become a slave, bound over to the service of human passion and greed.'[1]

The Pope, then, looks at these men who have gathered to themselves so much power, the men who hold all the strings of modern life in their hands, and the first thing that he notices is that there are only a few of them. There was an illustration of this in the papers a few weeks ago, at the time of the Railway-men's Wages Board enquiry. Mr. Walkden was giving evidence, and one thing he said was this :—

' When you look at *Who's Who* you see what's what. I see that the 82 directors (railway directors, he meant) hold 596 directorships between them . . . 30 of them are bank directors—four in the Bank of England. Thirty-two are directors of insurance companies, four of road-transport companies.'

And so on. That helps us to see what the Holy Father means when he says that ' these few men exercise in the economic sphere a domination that is despotic.'

[1] Much of this was repeated almost in the same words in the encyclical *Caritate Christi compulsi*, in the following year 1932.

The Holy Father goes on to speak of the irresistible power exercised by ' those who hold and control money ' ; that is to say, of course, any large financial business, insurance companies, and so on, but especially the banks, and more especially the central banks in the various countries. Most of us do not spend much time wondering about the nature of money ; we usually notice that we haven't enough of it. To-day especially it is evident that millions of people haven't got enough money ; plenty of things waiting to be bought, but no money to buy them with. Where does money come from, then ? Well, it is the ruler of a country who manufactures money and puts it into circulation, and nobody else must do it. Our coins are made by the Government (that is why the King's head is on them) and our paper money is printed by the Bank of England with the Government's authority and permission.

But these notes and coins are only one sort of money. During the last 100 years or so there has grown up the system of using cheques ; people pay each other with cheques, and most of the cheques are never changed into notes or coins at all, but simply credited to somebody's account in the books at the bank. So there is always this cheque money in existence—in fact, there is nine or ten times as much cheque money as there are banknotes and coins. It is not ' legal tender ' ; you can call it make-believe money if you life ; still, everybody does use it, and for practical purposes it is so much extra money.

Where does all that extra money come from ? It is created by the banks, when they make loans—

created out of nothing. When a bank lends you £1,000 to extend your business, the bank does not risk anything or sacrifice anything itself ; it does not have to hand over to you £1,000 in actual cash ; all it does is to make a little entry in its books, and then give you a cheque book.

A thousand pounds of new bank-money has come into existence by a stroke of the pen, and you are paying interest on it to the bank. That is what the Pope means when he says that the bankers ' are able also to govern credit, and decide to whom it shall be allotted.' That is to say, the ordinary banks decide whom they will lend their newly created money to ; and the Bank of England (or the corresponding central bank in other countries) turns the total stream of credit on and off at will by means of the ' bank rate.'[1]

So you see how all the money comes to us through the bankers ; and the bankers distribute it in the form of loans, to people who they think will make profit out of it and be able to pay them interest.

[1] Some people still find it difficult to understand the facts of credit-creation. What it comes to is this : During the last hundred years, but especially since 1914, bankers have been inventing a new and very useful sort of money which we may call bank-credit or cheque-money. Few cheques are actually cashed, they are mostly paid into banking accounts. There is very little cash in existence compared with the vast volume of bank deposits ; say, perhaps, 400 million as compared with 2,000 million. When a bank allows me an overdraft I pay it away in cheques which promptly become deposits in some bank or other. The cheque-system thus makes it possible for banks to lend more ' money ' (at least ten times more ' money ') than they really have. This power, which the ordinary banks use in subordination to the Bank of England, is called credit-creation ; a good and necessary thing in itself but too great a power to be turned to private profit and domination.

' They supply the life-blood, so to speak, to the entire economic body,' says the Pope.

In the Catholic Middle Ages they knew how to keep their moneylenders in order (Shakespeare's picture of Shylock shows us how moneylenders were regarded then), but to-day we put all power into their hands ; we allow them to do as they please about inflation and deflation—that is, decide how much money there shall be in circulation—and we take it for granted that everything must be done by a loan, and that everybody must be in debt to the bankers, one loan on top of another. ' They grasp in their hands the very soul of production,' says the Pope, ' so that no one dare breathe against their will.'

Remember that the bankers are not responsible to anybody. They use these powers, these simply enormous powers, not necessarily for the common good, but for their own purposes and profit. Even the Bank of England is simply a private company with its directors and its chairman elected by its own shareholders. It came into existence as a syndicate for lending money to the Government in the time of William III ; he gave it certain privileges in a Royal Charter, and the charter has to be renewed from time to time ever since.

Theoretically, the Bank of England's charter might be revoked. Perhaps you remember seeing a film about Disraeli ; how when he was Prime Minister the Bank of England refused to lend the Government the money to buy shares in the Suez Canal, and how Disraeli forced the Bank to lend it by threatening to revoke its charter. That was true enough, but it is not likely that a Prime Minister would talk in that way now.

It is the other way round now—in almost all countries it is the Central Bank that gives orders to the politicians, and the politicians do as they are told. So the Pope draws a picture for us of the financiers who 'struggle to acquire control of the State, so that its resources and authority may be made evil use of in the economic struggles.' 'The State,' he says, 'should be the supreme arbiter; it should rule in kingly fashion far above party contention; it should be intent only upon justice and the common good. Instead, it has become a slave bound over to the service of human passion and greed.'

Whichever way you look, you will see that our present troubles are caused or intensified by the greed of the bankers. Municipal houses, for instance —why must the rents be so high that people can't afford them? Simply because they are built by means of a loan, and the moneylenders must have their interest. Why doesn't this country use its land properly and begin to feed itself? Because the farmers are so hopelessly in debt to the banks that they can't carry on and are going bankrupt in hundreds.

Why has the whole country been crippled by over-taxation ever since the War? Chiefly to pay the interest on war loan. There was eight thousand million pounds of debt for the War, and most of it was imaginary money lent directly or indirectly to the Government by the banks. Perhaps three-quarters of it was taken up by the bankers and financiers and their clients without any risk to themselves or any cash payment—simply a piece of book-keeping, and they have been drawing their interest ever since, or else turning their bonds into cash by selling them to people like you and me : the most colossal piece of financial conjuring in the history of the world.[1]

Why must wages be reduced all round, and men be thrown out of work in thousands by machinery ? Because the big industries fall more and more into the power of the banks, and the banks think they can get a greater return on their capital if they reduce costs.

We live under economic dictatorship, says the Pope. ' The desire for profit has led to an unbridled ambition for power ; the economic side of life has become hard, cruel and relentless to a ghastly extent.'

Why must the unemployed have their maintenance cut down to starvation point ? Why are Courts of Referees and relief committees and suchlike out for saving money at all costs ? And all those domineering busybodies who so often find their way on to such committees—why are they having the

[1] By far the greater part of the War Loan was originally acquired, not by people who paid for it with their own savings, but in the following way. The banks wrote round to their favoured clients (especially to the moneylending houses, insurance companies and so on) and said in effect: ' We have the distributing of this War Loan. Will you take, say, £50,000 worth ? We are quite aware you haven't the money, but that doesn't matter, we will let you have an overdraft. Just write out a cheque on us and it will be honoured. The War Bonds then will be yours, but you will let us hold them as security for the overdraft. You will get 5 per cent War Loan interest, and when you have paid us 4 per cent interest on your overdraft you will still be 1 per cent to the good.'

time of their lives just now ? Simply because the nation has got to balance its budget. There is no particular reason why the nation should balance its budget. The nation is in quite a different position to a private individual.

If you go to Italy now, you'll find they are doing all kinds of wonderful things—new roads and railways everywhere, millions of acres of new land being made fit for cultivation, thousands of unemployed being set up on the land with new farms, whole new towns are being built—life and hope and energy all over the country ; but Mussolini makes no pretence of balancing his budget.

When the bankers say the nation must balance its budget, what they mean is that the nation must pay them their interest, no matter who suffers.

We have all noticed the outward sign of banking prosperity since the War, the handsome new bank buildings that have been going up in every town. And we need not be surprised to find that now, in the midst of general depression and poverty, the banks are still prospering. To the moneylender, the misfortunes of his neighbour are just one more source of profit. Last week the Big Five Banks were declaring their annual dividends. Their total profits were over eight millions, and after making plentiful provision for bad debts, increased reserves, new buildings and so on, they declare dividends of 12 per cent, 14, 15, 16 and 18 per cent.[1]

[1] This passage was read by some readers quite mistakenly as meaning that the five joint-stock banks are chiefly to blame for all our troubles. It should be understood that the banking system in this country has roughly four parts to it : the Bank of

There is no need to picture our all-powerful financiers as monsters of wickedness and cruelty. The Pope is not inclined to let them off too lightly. He says that under the present system the power falls into the hands of ' those only who are the strongest, which often means those who fight most ruthlessly and pay least heed to the dictates of conscience.' Still, I think we might say that bankers are ordinary average men like you and me, clever enough in their own narrow business of money-lending, and rather stupid and unimaginative about everything else. At present I am sure they are feeling rather appalled and bewildered at the state they've got the world into. They probably have no idea what to do next—in fact the Governor of the Bank of England said as much a few weeks ago. The one thing they certainly will do is to hold on as tenaciously as possible to their present power over the rest of mankind.

That vast and irresponsible power is exactly what they ought not to have, according to our holy Father the Pope, and you may expect to hear the Church protesting against it more and more. When things were going well enough it seemed hardly the Church's business to protest—if men were content to be ruled by bankers why should the Church interfere ? But it's a different thing altogether now, when the bankers are snatching the food away, as it

England, the private merchant banks, the discount houses and money-market, and the joint-stock banks. The joint-stock banks may fairly be called the most useful and least harmful, but in monetary policy they have no choice but to follow the Bank of England.

were, from the lips of the poor, and tearing the shoes off the feet of the children. ' It is a violation of right order,' says the Pope, ' when Labour is used by Capital in such a way that all the activity of industry is diverted to the arbitrary advantage of Capital, regardless of the human dignity of the workers, regardless of the social character of economic life, regardless of social justice, regardless of the common good.'

Our Blessed Lord has put it all into half a dozen words : ' You cannot serve God and Mammon.' We have been trying to do it. We have put money on the throne of God, and there it reigns, mysterious and supreme, demanding human sacrifice. We have served Mammon and now we have got what we deserved. The only way to save ourselves is to dethrone that false god and set ourselves once more to do the Will of our Father who is in Heaven.

RIGHT USES OF CREDIT-CREATION[1]

WE are hearing a good deal about houses just at present.

Immense plans on foot—all the slum areas throughout England to be cleared in the next five years and replaced with decent houses. The Government tells the local authorities to get on with it at once ; Sir Austen Chamberlain says that conditions in Birmingham make his blood boil ; the Archbishop of Canterbury says that the time has come to remove this scandal from our social life ; the Prince of Wales says that we can't afford to have slums because they are centres of disease, ill-health and discontent.

Well, that's splendid, of course. Those are just the things that lesser people have been saying ever since you and I were born. If the nation is really in a mood to do it at last, let us thank God with all our hearts.

And where is the money to come from ? That is the tactless sort of question that must not be asked on these occasions, but let us ask it all the same. ' You must borrow the money,' says the Government.

' Money is cheap now, the moneylenders can't

[1] This was part of a sermon, Holy Family Church, Birmingham, May 21, 1933.

12

find borrowers, so just at present they are willing to take less interest than usual. Seize the opportunity for a loan, and let the nation attack the housing problem in the same spirit as it won the war.'

Just so. And if you have a good memory you will know how much interest we are still paying on account of the War. Isn't it somewhere near two hundred millions a year ? It is that load of interest and taxation which paralyses industry and causes so much misery.

And now we are invited (once more in the name of patriotism) to stoop down while these money-lenders fasten upon our backs another great burden of interest, another set of heavy chains to bind us to the service of Mammon.

' Stoke-on-Trent's programme of slum-clearance,' says the *Birmingham Post*, ' is now complete, and provides for dealing with twenty-five acres in the Potteries at the rate of five acres a year. The cost . . . is well over £1,000,000. The burden on the ratepayers will be heavy, but work will be provided for a large number of unemployed men.'

Let us try to be clear about this money business ; the essence of it is simple enough, although they try to make it seem complicated. Where do the loans come from for such purposes as this ? From the banks of one sort and another, with the Bank of England at their back.

Where do the banks, the Bank of England itself, where does it get the money from to lend ? It doesn't get it from anywhere, it just creates it out of nothing ; what they call a ' new issue of credit,' and the other banks do the same in their degree, creating the money they lend, cancelling it when it is repaid, drawing the interest upon it in between.

Has a bank any right in justice to take interest, real interest, on money so created ? No right whatever. But that is the financial system of this country, built up gradually by this private company of moneylenders called the Bank of England, which without being responsible to anybody is the real government of the country.

All our present troubles and injustices can be traced back to their causes in the financial system, a system which most of the other countries have by this time copied from us. We talk about the anti-God campaign in Russia, and it is a dreadful thing in all conscience. But probably in the sight of heaven the greatest enemy of God and man on this earth during the last hundred years has been the Bank of England.

That is not necessarily a personal accusation against those who control the Bank of England. Certainly they have nothing to be proud of in their conduct since 1914, but they are not alone in that. We cannot be sure how far they have understood what they are doing, and how far they are just the creatures of a tradition and a machine.

The function they perform—of creating money and credit—is in itself a noble function and one which rightly belongs to the King. It supplies the economic life-blood of the community, says our Holy Father the Pope.

What a wonderful thing the power of creating

credit could be if it were used for the common good ; if only it were not diverted to narrow private ends of profit and domination ! It could be in the fullest sense a creative and life-giving power, a reflection of God's own creative generosity.

By creations of credit, or loans free of interest, not only could the slums be cleared away, but every family in England could live in a good up-to-date house at a reasonable rent. Credit power used creatively would go far to solve all those human problems that arise out of unemployment and enforced leisure.

It could be used to make the world safe for children, encouraging parents to have a normal family and opening up the full possibilities of education. Not only slums and their sad consequences, but all the other effects of poverty—so many crimes and diseases and vices that flourish merely because men and women are in desperate poverty—all these could be attacked and overcome in like manner, perhaps not all in five years, but in our lifetime. We might live to see a new world if only we could learn to use money instead of letting it use us.

Well, the upshot of all this as regards housing is that I shall begin to believe that the Government is in earnest when they persuade the Bank of England to issue a great loan without interest to enable the local authorities to set to work.

St James in to-day's epistle tells us what he means by ' religion clean and undefiled before God and man.' St James, you remember, presided over the Church at Jerusalem, that primitive society of the Christians who had joined at Pentecost, the men and women who had listened to our Lord Himself. You remember what they did—they put all their money and goods into one common stock.

That wasn't an essential part of the Faith—it was never introduced anywhere outside Jerusalem—and even in Jerusalem it did not work successfully for long from a practical point of view. But they had the right spirit. It was worth doing, for it tells us more than anything else perhaps about the spirit of our Lord's teaching and the things He had laid stress on.

Those first Christians each felt that they couldn't bear the idea of being comfortably off themselves while any of their brethren were in need. That was most certainly our Lord's spirit, and the spirit we need to-day. ' Doers of the word and not hearers only.'

MODERN USURY

SOME Catholics propose the abolition of all interest on loans, but I cannot see any way out of our difficulties in that direction.

In the first place there is surely not the remotest possibility of ever getting such a change enacted into law, and it seems a pity to waste useful energy on working for it.

In the second place, the abolition of interest would not make much difference to the real power of the moneylenders, which comes, as the Pope says, from their power to control credit, and decide who is to receive it. Their inside knowledge of what they are going to do next gives them all the opportunities they need of getting rich by manipulating prices and by investment. As for pure interest derived from loans, it is comparatively a small matter, and one can even imagine them renouncing it if necessary in order to keep their real power.

In the third place, the abolition of interest can hardly be advocated on moral grounds at this time of day. Catholic theologians have long agreed that although money was not fruitful in the Middle Ages, it must be regarded as fruitful in our own times, and therefore interest can always be charged for a loan whether productive or not. They would say (what is quite undeniable, I think) that the immense material changes since the Renaissance—the mariner's compass, the invention of printing, the discoveries of science and their application, the ever-rising standard of comfort and civilised living, in short, the unlimited expansion of production—have created a world in which there is always a profitable investment waiting for the limited amount of gold and silver which is called money, and consequently the lender of money is always entitled to interest to compensate him for the use he might otherwise have made of it. This principle is clearly admitted, by the way, in the new Code of Canon Law, canon 1543.

In two respects, however, the theologians (as far as my limited acquaintance with them goes) do not seem to have kept themselves fully informed of the rapid developments of modern finance. They are inclined to think of money as necessarily metallic, hardly realising that modern business can only be carried on by a system of paper money and cheques far in excess of any possible gold or silver backing ; consequently they are not alive to the danger of the moneylender getting his fingers on the issue of currency at its very source.

Still more serious, the theologians, like nearly everybody else, have still to notice that there is such a thing as credit-creation. Credit-creation in private hands has two bad effects. First it makes it quite easy for the moneylender to get interest on money which does not exist at all except on his books ; or (an alternative description of the same thing) to get interest ten times over on the same money at the same time. The classic example of credit-creation is

the four War Loans.   Secondly it is the machinery
by which the moneylender plays his perpetual game
of raising and lowering prices at his own will and for
his own advantage.

Interest then cannot be called unlawful in itself,
and we may safely say that a thing which is
sanctioned both by the Catholic Code of Canon Law
and by the financial code of Soviet Russia[1] is perhaps
not likely to be abolished.   Interest evidently becomes unlawful when it is excessive, and I suppose
even a low interest can be excessive when it is allowed
to come before elementary human rights, as, for
instance, when debenture shareholders are paid out
of an industry which is not paying a living wage to
its workpeople.   Also I cannot see how the charge
of unlawful usury can be evaded in those financial
operations which now control the issue of money so
that it comes into existence always in the form of a
debt.   And the same has to be said, it seems to me,
of all interest charged for overdrafts or new issues

---

[1] For purposes of credit-issue the Soviet has two banking
institutions, Gosbank and Prombank.   Gosbank is responsible
for providing short-terms loans to business (State business, of
course), in the ordinary way.   Interest is paid on these, and also
on those loans for various purposes to which the Soviet citizen is
often invited to subscribe.   But initial credit for capital production (e.g. the building of a new factory or of houses, etc.), is
provided by Prombank free of interest and free of repayment,
the only charges made being a commission of one per mille, and an
annual sum from the factory for depreciation.   When the factory
sells its goods to the public Prombank will be recouped, so to
speak, by a State tax on the turnover of the new factory, anything
from 2 per cent to 50 per cent.   In other words, credit for new
production is issued not in the form of a loan, with its dead
weight of debt and interest or debenture shares, but in the form
of a State investment, a genuine investment which shares the
risk of failure.

c

of credit, except perhaps the small interest that would represent banking expenses. But the greatest crime of the modern usurer seems to be the deliberate manipulation of prices through the alternating expansion and contraction of credit.

THE GOLD IDOL

THERE is no shortage of Myrrh this year ; you might almost say it suffers from over-production. Frankincense, too, is readily available, if not always in the finer grades. But Gold—ah, Gold is another matter. Modern kings are not allowed to be generous with Gold. Mammon has first call on it. Mammon is sitting tight on it. Mammon is hoping to find a use for it again, even yet. His worshippers still need an idol, and nothing has ever filled that need so conveniently as Gold.

Gold has stood—not always and everywhere, indeed, but generally, and more and more the last four hundred years—for Money and Power. For gold men have fought bloody wars ; for gold they have risked their lives, thousands at a time, in strange desert places ; for gold men have been willing to sell their souls·and commit every possible crime.

Gold has its own temples and its own priests and its own shrines underground in great cities.

Gold has its human sacrifices, too. More human sacrifices than any other idol ever had. You will find them in workhouses, where so many helpless and dreary lives are dragging to a close without ever having had a chance of happiness. You will find them in prisons, where eight thousand men and women are put every year simply for lack of money, and where even the real criminals mostly become so through poverty.

You will find these human sacrifices in greatest number in the slums, where infant mortality rises to such high percentages as compared with residential quarters, and where life is a stunted and poisoned and embittered growth for hundreds of thousands who are just as capable of happiness as any others. You will find them in hospitals, and casual wards, and Salvation Army shelters, and suicide-mortuaries—all the places where there are men and women and children that are broken and done to death because they have no money.

Men worship an idol because they think there is life and power in it, but when the idol is overthrown its power is seen to be nothing. So it is with Gold to-day. Everybody can see that it was a deception, and that all those victims are being offered up to a fraud.

Ordinary people are coming to see that money can be spiritualised, so to speak. The more it can be made to depend on social confidence and co-operation, the better it is. Paper notes representing gold are therefore a better currency than gold itself. Still better are paper notes representing not gold but goods. Best of all might be a system where all payments were made by cheque.

When money was gold, there was some excuse for letting poverty go on. Kings and Governments had to borrow money from those who held it, the gold-owners. They borrowed it on the strength of the nation's future productivity. Now that the gold-delusion is over, and money is no longer gold, there is no possible excuse for the continuance of poverty. No excuse for the Governments which continue to borrow the ' money ' which they could just as easily create for themselves on the same strength of the nation's plentiful productivity. And then everyone could have their fair share (as Catholic teaching has always demanded) of what the earth produces.

The brief world-reign of the gold-owners is ending, thank God.

The Gold idol lies overthrown. All the priests and scribes of Mammon are clustering round it, trying to lift it up again, warning us of what will happen if we cease worshipping it. Liars and dupes—why should anybody take notice of them, even if they own the whole Press ?

In this year 1934 there is only one issue for those who understand : to end the insane and murderous money-system which now dominates all the world and poisons every department of human life. It is the time when all men must make their choice, whether they will turn to God from idols, to serve the living and true God.

January 1934.

MONEY AND THE LAND

PRESIDENT ROOSEVELT'S new Declaration of Independence is as sure of its place in history as the other one. He has set out to make money do its job as a means of exchanging goods. Somehow or other he is going to make it work ' for the welfare of all the people.' A notable phrase. It is a long time since ' the welfare of all the people ' has been a consideration in the minds of those who create and control money.

When a man has fallen into the hands of a money-lender—the sort of moneylender who forces you to borrow again to pay the interest owing on his previous loan—the first and most urgent thing to be done is to get the man out of those clutches.

That is exactly the plight of our own country. The Government of England carries on by borrowing, and is always deeply in debt.

The debt is not a debt of actual cash or gold, but a sort of enormous overdraft of imaginary money. Imaginary money ('bank credit ') is good enough for the purpose, because very little of it will ever need to come into use further than the cheque stage.

Couldn't the Government use the nation's credit to make real or imaginary money for itself, instead of going to the moneylender ? It could, and of course, it ought to ; but it chooses to keep on going to the moneylender. And hence the difficulties about balancing the budget, hence the heavy taxation that cripples industry, hence the false ' economy ' which drives men out of employment and then slowly starves them.

Money is not a god that it should rule the lives of men. Money should be simply a means of exchange to be managed for men's convenience. It is for the Government to issue enough money to enable the country to produce what it needs and to buy what it produces.

That much, at any rate, is already clear to President Roosevelt. Inevitably, as time goes on, the implications will become clear, and he will have to master the moneylenders or be mastered by them.

Credit (says Pope Pius XI) is the very life-blood of the community. When it is juggled with for private ends, millions of men and women and children are going to suffer ; to suffer not merely inconvenience or worry, but actual shortage of food, clothing, warmth and shelter, in a world where all these necessities of life are abundant. That is what is happening at present.

The attitude we adopt in face of our neighbours' lack of the ordinary necessities of life is the one great test insisted on by Christ our Lord.

Did He mean this test to apply to ecclesiastics as well as to laity ? He did. What will He have to say to us when we have watched in silence the oppression of the poor ? That remains to be seen.

The big moneylenders are breaking the seventh and tenth commandments on the grandest possible scale. That is why credit reform is an urgent matter of elementary justice to which no Catholic has a right to profess indifference.

There are, indeed, things more fundamental than money. Catholics, being instinctively historical and realistic, are naturally inclined to a back-to-the-land solution of economic problems. But for land cultivation, even more than for factory production, there is needed plenty of capital and a beneficent system of credit.

In the *Morning Post* of July 5, it was stated that 90 per cent of Norfolk and Suffolk farmers are insolvent. ' The farmers in these afflicted regions have exhausted their credit, and their overdrafts are looked upon as a bad debt. This is the more unfortunate as modern knowledge opens out new opportunities to farmers with capital.'

Back-to-the-land movements without credit reform must necessarily be a ' wash-out.'

Mussolini has put thousands of men on the land and announces that Italy can now grow all the wheat she needs. But meanwhile his budget deficit keeps on growing and growing. Ultimately Mussolini, too, will have to face up to the moneylenders.

The more you look into things the more you see that no measure of social justice can be attained in any direction until the robes of power have been stripped from the moneylender and he is seen for what he is.

He will not surrender without a struggle. But no class war can be preached on this issue, for every class alike stands to gain when the nation's credit is used for ' the welfare of all the people.'

July 1933.

MONEY AND SLUM-CLEARANCE

A MAN in Sheffield writes to me : ' Have you all only one topic in variations—the Banks ! ' I can understand his irritation. All this criticism and indignation—even if it is justified, what good does it do ?

No good, I admit, if there is no hope of what the Pope calls ' social justice.' If the sufferings of the people must continue for another lifetime or two, then a regular supply of opium would be more to the point than any teaching about justice. But if the right and just way is all the time straight in front of our noses—

Here are the reasons, then, why we must keep on about the evil side of the banking system.

First, because it is the point that the Pope starts from. Only it is no use merely repeating the Pope's few sentences like a parrot. He expects us to show how they fit the actual circumstances.

Secondly, because the good possibilities about credit and money are not yet realised, and the only way of having them realised is to show the immense power of money and credit in the hands of their present controllers. Power for evil mostly ; but it might just as well be power for good.

Take Housing again. The Government's Five Year Plan for ending slums is fading out in a feeble

eruption of posters and face-saving speeches. The
latest idea is for 200,000 unfit houses to come down
during the five years (Birmingham alone has 40,000
back-to-back houses), and the Minister has begun to
use the blessed word ' re-conditioning.'

To put it in a nutshell, the great Plan will come to
nothing because the Local Authorities have refused
to ` be driven to the moneylenders. Slums or no
slums, they know they are deep enough in debt
already.

Birmingham's debt totals 53 million pounds,
involving ' loan charges ' which represent 4s. 7d.
on the rates. According to the elective auditors,
the City Treasurer thinks the time has come when
non-reproductive expenditure should be met entirely
out of income, but ' assumes that we shall be bur-
dened *for all time* with the present indebtedness, even
if at a lower rate of interest.' (Italics mine.)

The banker's paradise—a world in which debts
can never be paid off !

As things are, the Slum-clearance Plan is (perhaps
unconsciously for most of those concerned) simply
the handiest dodge for reviving business in the Street
of the Moneylenders.

But all this time the slums are there. So are plenty
of pickaxes and spades, and plenty of land, and
plenty of clay for bricks, and plenty of other
materials, and two millions of men waiting to be
allowed to work. Nothing wanting to set the vast
machine moving except the economic lubrication
called money.

And the only reason for that lack is because the

Bank of England decrees that all money must come into existence as a debt ; and because the King's Government, which once found such an arrangement a convenience, miserably allows it still to go on when it has long ago become a calamity and a disaster for England and the world.

November, 1933.

ENGLAND UNDER THE MEANS TEST

THE other day the Government stated its
determination to go on depriving some of the
unemployed—those longest out of work and in
direst need of help—of their medical insurance and
maternity benefit.

The Minister of Health, while defending this
decision in Parliament, let fall a remark which he
no doubt regarded as a commonplace, but which
ought to have been challenged at once.

'The real remedy for these admitted evils,' he
said, ' is in the general improvement of trade,
industry, and employment.'

Well, that is an utter fallacy. The old foreign
trade of this country (for that is what he meant, of
course) has mostly gone for ever. There can be no
' general improvement ' of that kind on a scale
sufficiently large to solve the unemployment
problem.

Why not face the facts ? The foreigners have
learned to make for themselves the things we used
to sell them. They, too, have a surplus to export.
Our former customers have become rival manu-
facturers.

If we try to live now on our export trade we are
going to starve.

Besides, even if trade does improve it will never

do away with unemployment now. Unemployment comes from our increased power over nature, just as much as from bad trade. More machinery, more power-production ; less work for men. Trade returns have been showing some steady improvement for months, and yet the number of permanent unemployed has shown a steady increase too.

Another fact to be faced, then : Unemployment is inevitable. It need not be a curse. It could be a blessing, if there were any social justice. The right way with unemployment (as the Pope told the Unemployed Pilgrimage) is to see in it an opportunity for learning a noble use of leisure.

Meanwhile, here is our Bankers' Government snatching the last shilling or two from the destitute men and women who have been sticking it for three years with such marvellous patience in the front trenches of the Depression. Maternity benefit, even. Let the poor law look after them ! ' The real remedy for these admitted evils is in the general improvement of trade.'

No, the ' real remedy ' for evils of that kind is for the rest of the nation to stand by the unemployed.

' Only a few of our fellow-citizens are hungry and ragged.' Somebody said this to me the other day.

Well, let us look at the evidence. I mean evidence available to the general public.

Last month the Minister of Health spoke in the House of Commons about the effects of the depression on the nation's health. He said that the general *physical* health (as distinct from mental health) was normal in spite of the depression, but he had received bad reports from certain areas (including Lancashire and Birmingham) which needed careful attention.

Quite a lot of our fellow-citizens live in Lancashire and Birmingham.

Still using careful language, the Minister of Health said there was little or no direct evidence of ill-health attributable to malnutrition, but localised areas showed some harmful effects, including West Cumberland, Tyneside, Hartlepool, Sunderland, and some of the mining areas.

These official admissions on the part of the Means Test Government are illuminated by several other organised enquiries which have published results during this year (1933).

The medical officers of health at Deptford, from a study of numerous families, declared that ' there are to-day many homes in which, after the rent is paid and allowance made for heating and clothing, there is an insufficient sum available for food '— only about 4s. a head per week in fact, not enough to ensure the minimum varied diet recommended by the Ministry of Health in their publications.

Five to six shillings is reckoned by doctors the minimum cost of food for one person. Another doctor, writing in the *Observer*, gave the following instances, supplied by medical officers from various localities, of people living on ' half-rations ' : Hammersmith, 2s. 4d., 2s. 8d., 1s. 11d., 3s. 11d., 1s. 7d. ; Stockton-on-Tees, 2s. 10½d. ;   London, 2s. 5½d. ; Glamorgan, 1s. 8d. ; Rotherham, 1s. 9d.

A Sheffield Social Survey Committee visited 3,273 households, and found one-fifth of them on or below the poverty line ; but, taking the children only, the proportion was much greater—one-third in fact. This report concerns the period 1931–32, before the full introduction of the Means Test and the other panic economy measures. ' Conditions must be more difficult now,' remarks *The Times*.

Finally, there is the highly authoritative report lately issued by the Save the Children Fund. Longmans publish it under the title of *Unemployment and the Children* (2s. 6d.).

According to this investigation, under-nourishment is the chief problem. The flat rate of 2s. per child unemployment benefit is quite inadequate. If the rent is over 5s. (which, of course, it practically always is), under-nourishment is unavoidable. Little deterioration was noticed in children between 1927–31, but there was marked deterioration between 1931 and 1932. Clothing, too, had deteriorated. (This report also is about pre-Means Test days.)

All the investigations about children make it clear that the situation has been largely retrieved by free meals for school-children. But this does not help children under five, nor children at secondary schools (who are special sufferers from the unemployment in their family) ; and even for the school-attenders there are the holidays when free meals usually stop. Moreover, out of 317 local authorities during 1931–32, only 157 used their free-meal powers ; and of these the practice varied from providing full meals to providing a mere half-pint of milk per day.

One M.O. notes that by the time a young child shows signs of malnutrition irreparable damage has been done already. Another says that in cases of unemployment it is the mother of the family who goes short.

Other doctors observe that prolonged ill-nourishment leads to a well-recognised condition of loss of vitality, anæmia, unhealthy skin appearance, ' poor blood,' chronic colds and a liability to catch any infection.

Yes. After semi-starvation comes *pestilence*.

' Only a few of our fellow-citizens are ragged and hungry.' Does this really square with the published evidence, or with the evidence of our own eyes ?

Any such easy-going acceptance of poverty of this kind is a mental survival from the past ages of scarcity. The ages of scarcity are over, or ought to be. We live in August, 1933, when President Roosevelt is preparing to pay farmers for *not* growing wheat, and when a million and a half oranges are thrown into the sea at Liverpool.

If anybody in England is hungry and ragged, somebody must be diverting industrial activity to their own advantage, as the Pope says, regardless of social justice.

' Everybody in England shall have a fair share of the necessities of life.' Why not adopt such a watchword as that, on which not only moralists and new-economists, but also old-economists and even practical politicians could conceivably unite.

After all it would not be much of a change. What with unemployment pay, poor relief, old age pensions, etc., we are nearly doing it already, but in a grudging Poor-law-spirited fashion.

After that we might see our way more easily. When things are on the mend it is practical to look for some principle that is unmistakably God's will to be done, and hold on to that, accepting its implications as they come into view. Then things are likely to straighten out as we go on.

Such a principle at present seems to be the right of every human being to the necessities of life in an age of plenty. If the nation would make up its mind to stand by the unemployed to that extent, it would begin to see light.

Autumn, 1933.

D

MAKING UNEMPLOYMENT A MARTYRDOM

A FEW days ago as I was saying the Mass of the Oxford Martyrs, two words suddenly seemed to jump out at me. 'Great tribulation.' They were the words so much on the lips of the Pope when he spoke to the unemployed from England. This must have been the text, then, that came into his mind at the sight of the men from the silent factories of the Tyneside or Lancashire : 'Who are these, and whence do they come ? These are they who have come from the Great Tribulation ! ' With all his love for a well-accommodated text, I wonder if the Holy Father knew that he was quoting from the Mass of Edmund Campion and his companion Martyrs of England ?

Certainly there was nothing unfitting in that. Almost indeed he might have greeted them, as other young Englishmen were greeted by the Roman saint, with *Salvete flores martyrum*.

For unemployment, in this country where the town-population has been so completely torn up from any roots on the land, is indeed a martyrdom, in the sufferings it brings, in the patience with which they are endured, and most of all in that which is usually the martyr's bitterest trial—the suspicion and resentment of his own fellow-countrymen.

The attitude can be noted in a phrase used the

other day in Parliament by the Minister of Labour.
Any assistance given to the unemployed man outside
insurance (he said) is ' at the expense of the man's
fellow-citizens and fellow-workers.'

A common enough point of view, but how mean
and ignorant and ungenerous and untrue ! If the
unemployed have to be assisted ' at the expense '
of the employed, the only reason is because the King's
Government leaves the nation's money-supply in
the hands of a gang of private moneylenders.

The country can produce plenty of what is needed
for employed and unemployed alike, and if the
unemployed had money to buy what they need it
need be ' at the expense ' of nobody but for everybody's gain.

The longer a man is unemployed, the more assistance he needs, and the less he gets.

As the weeks and months go on, clothes and boots
wear out, savings disappear, rent and insurance fall
behind, belongings are sold or pawned or taken away
by the hire-purchase firm, health suffers, difficulties
accumulate all round.   Meanwhile at every stage
in this process the financial authorities are busy
whittling down the unemployed man's income,
adding new injuries to his self-respect, pushing him
down further into helpless destitution.

Without pretending to be expert in all the ins
and outs of the endless regulations of our national
Bumbledom, anybody can observe the main lines of
the process.

First comes the regular unemployment insurance
pay : little enough in amount, never really intended

to do more than tide a man over a few weeks of bad luck. After six months of that comes the change to transitional benefit with its accompanying Means Test, under which, if any other members of the household are earning money, the out-of-work may find his ' labour-pay ' reduced or taken away altogether, until the family income is brought down as the law demands to the Poor-law level of subsistence.

Supposing he continues to receive something, the next stage will be when the arbiters of his fate decide that he is no longer likely to obtain insurable employment, and he is transferred to the Public Assistance proper. This means that he must definitely be in a state of destitution, total or partial, to qualify for receiving assistance. Hitherto, as a kind of symbol of independence, he had been allowed to keep his savings, if any, to the extent of say £10 in the savings-bank (the amount varies with locality). Now (except for a concession of a few pounds which has become usual in the last two years) that has to go, together with anything else that stands between him and the obligatory ' destitution.' His assistance may mostly be groceries, etc., instead of money. He may be worried by ' visitors ' into selling his wireless-set and so forth, though strictly speaking he cannot be compelled to. He will incur the censure of stern ecclesiastical moralists for spending twopence on an afternoon at the pictures.

If he is a lad without a home, and through a run of bad luck has given up his regular rooms to go into some registered lodging-house, he will find that the only public assistance available to him is a ticket for the workhouse.

Here is a simple illustration, from one locality, of how the burden of the unemployed man is made the heavier the longer he is out of work. During the first six months—ordinary insurance benefit—the unemployed man is allowed to do some paid work, outside ordinary working hours, up to the amount of let us say 3s. 6d. a week. When he drops to transitional benefit he is obliged to declare any money earned in that way, and it may be ' taken into account ' in the Means Test. And when he is ' thrown off the Labour ' on to the Poor Law, he has to declare it, with the knowledge that the whole amount will be deducted from his relief.

Out of his tiny income (even if it has been wiped out altogether by the family Means Test) the unemployed man is expected to find ninepence a week for health-insurance stamps, and naturally this becomes harder to keep up the longer he is out of work. When he is twelve months in arrears he loses right to sick benefit and his wife's maternity benefit.

On a certain day in 1934, the unemployed who are four years in arrears—mostly the elderly men ruthlessly scrapped by the industrial system—will lose their right to panel-doctor's treatment and (in some cases apparently) their right to old-age pension at sixty-five.[1]

[1] Two correspondents wrote to say that this and the preceding paragraph were in some respects inaccurate   They may have been, though I have not been able to ascertain exactly how or when or where   In any case, the inaccuracies alleged were not such as to affect the main facts or the argument drawn from them.

The Unemployment Assistance Board (if the new Bill gets through) will assist the ' genuine working man ' (so the Minister of Labour says) ' without the traditional stigma of the Poor-law.' Will the new system be any better than the old ? It could be. But you don't change a system merely by changing names. The new Board will be run by the same old Government, at the dictation of the same old Treasury, with the same old Bank of England giving its orders in the background.

Besides, if there is a ' traditional stigma of the Poor Law,' why should *any* unemployed, able-bodied or otherwise, or any other decent Englishmen or Englishwomen, be subjected to such needless martyrdom at all ?

Let us try to hold in our heads the simple fact that the ages of scarcity are over, and that for the first time in history there is plenty to go round. Unless we grasp this point we are not fitted even to begin the discussion of what social justice means to-day. And if we refuse to grasp it and to face its moral consequences, we are assuredly assisting in the re-crucifixion of Jesus Christ in the person of these His brethren.

December 15, 1933.

THE RIGHT TO THE NECESSARIES
OF LIFE

FROM Miss M. D. Leys, at the C.S.G. Summer School a couple of weeks ago, came a much-needed word of wisdom. She insisted on a clear distinction being drawn between the necessaries and the luxuries of life. Moreover, it seems she insisted also that this distinction must play a large part in solving the present economic troubles of the world.

The old economics placed too little emphasis on the distinction between luxuries and necessaries ; and the new economics, which ought to know better, sometimes tends to the same mistake.

Supply, demand, production, consumption, goods, exchange of goods—yes, but hardly anybody stops to ask *what* goods ? What things are most truly to be called wealth ? What things should have priority in production and distribution ?

Ruskin used to ask such questions, but the professionals were not likely to interrupt their discussions to listen to a mere art-critic.

In our Lord's teaching (if that is of any interest to economists) the distinction between necessities and luxuries is all-pervading. Our Lord says in effect : Every member of God's human family has a right to have the necessities of human life, and the wise will desire to have no more.

It is no use preaching the second of these truths without the first.

You baptise a baby these days—' Peter John, go in peace and the Lord be with you '—and a few weeks later you discover that Peter John is rapidly fading away. Malnutrition, says the welfare doctor in a note ; mother not well-nourished enough to feed Peter John properly. Transitional labour-money at the relief-scale stage, father, mother, the two children, twenty shillings a week ; rent eight shillings ; no margin for milk, so to speak. What about some official milk, with the help of the welfare note ? ' Everybody else has got to manage—you must manage too. Better take it to the Such-and-such Society.' The such-and-such (local organised charity) grants perhaps one week's milk and then stops it for lack of funds.

Meanwhile Peter John has surveyed this world for ten weeks and found it not too good. He is evidently preparing to look for a better one unless somebody, officially or unofficially, gives him more definite encouragement to remain.

Well, of course, Mr. Neville Chamberlain's next Budget, with its hundreds of millions debt charges and what not, has to be balanced and Peter John must do his bit towards it like everybody else.

Peter John's contribution seems likely to be disproportionate to his size.

From God's point of view there is plenty of milk for Peter John and Peter John's mother. Overproduction, in fact, our Government would call it. Lots of it is fed to pigs, and lots of it is poured down drains. To get the surplus milk conveyed direct to the poor without injuring the milk trade would be a complicated and impossible task.

There is a more simple and natural way—give the poor enough money to buy the milk they need. Call it ' purchasing-power ' by all means, if you think it sounds better that way.

At our present state of civilisation, as long as it lasts, milk ought to be as easy to get as water. In towns pure water is practically free ; not really free —my own water-rate is getting on for 2s. a week— but as near free as makes no matter. Sister Water, most humble, serviceable, precious, pure—nobody in England need be without that necessity of life.

Milk ought to be as freely available as water. Bread also. Potatoes, perhaps, and other such things that God makes easy to produce. Clothing certainly, and fuel in English winters. The time has arrived when the right to the necessities of life should be disconnected from work and wages. Justice demands it, and common sense too.

President Roosevelt is trying to create adequate purchasing-power through wages alone. It is inconceivable that he can succeed in this, and every student of the new economics is wondering what will be the President's next step towards consumer-credit.

In England we are familiar enough with the idea of consumer-credit in various private forms of discount, Co-op. ' divvy,' bonus, and so on. Moreover, we already have the ' labour pay,' the poor-law relief, the old-age pension, widows' pensions, free meals for schoolchildren, pensions for Cabinet Ministers and poet-laureates and policemen, and so on and so forth. Why not do the thing with a good grace, and have frankly a national dividend that would guarantee the necessities of life to all, work or no work ?

By all means see that everybody, rich or poor, does some work, if you can think of anything for them to do. But the duty of work is one thing and the right to the necessaries of life is another.

There is no earthly reason why money should be so scarce, so lacking to those who need it most desperately, except that it happens to suit the moneylenders who, by the most remarkable arrangement the world has ever known, are also the money-creators.

August, 1933.

THE NECESSITY OF WORK

THE beauty and holiness of work, of work that is done willingly and with joy. That (one would say) was the central thought in the Holy Father's talk to the unemployed.

Holy Scripture pictures for us the first days of man, how God placed him in the garden of pleasure ' to dress it and keep it.' His material needs were safely provided for, for the rest he was a gardener and his work was a joy. Then came his sin, and work was turned into an unwilling drudgery. ' Cursed is the earth in thy work, with labour and toil shalt thou eat thereof all the days of thy life.'

And so even now (says the Pope) the world is blind to the holiness of work, turns it into something soul-destroying rather than salvation. The preaching of class-war, the concentration of money-power into a few hands, the servitude of the workers, the worship of production as a god, the abolition of the social rest-days ordained by God—these are the symptoms which show how deeply the idea of work has been poisoned by the sin of man.

But it need not be so, the Holy Father goes on, for Jesus Christ who restored all things has restored also the dignity and the holiness of work. He was born in a working-class family, He was known as the son of the carpenter, He earned His own living with His own sacred Hands. From the Holy Family we may rediscover that work is not only full of dignity and holiness but also full of joy, when it is done willingly for those we love.

' Great tribulation,' the Pope called it, to be without work, as so many millions are to-day. ' We never value a thing until we have lost it.' Through the tribulation God is teaching the world the lesson that work is noble and desirable.

Even the drudgery that men hated they long to have back now, since it meant livelihood. But it will never come back. There never will be again the ancient necessity for countless myriads of ever-toiling hands. The work that was done in olden times by terrorised slaves and serfs and in modern times by a dispossessed and discontented proletariat, will in future be done by the energy of Nature which man has learned to control.

To that extent the curse of Adam has worked itself out, and the disappearance of drudgery brings into full relief what the Pope is not afraid to call the *necessity of work*. Man cannot do without it. And yet he needs to be *free* even in his work.

There is the problem for our generation. Jesus Christ shows us how to abolish slavery, and we must apply His teaching and that of His Vicar. We have to learn all over again the beauty and holiness of willing work : we have to find out how to *make* work for ourselves. Joyful work. Work worth doing. And above all, of course, we must ensure that all men, women and children, have their rightful share, work or no work, of what God's beautiful earth provides for all.

' Great tribulation,' indeed, for those who have to endure such physical and mental suffering, such frustrations of their elementary natural human rights, while the more comfortable rest of us are slowly and stolidly, with every kind of mental resistance and reluctance, being forced by circumstances along the unaccustomed path that leads to social justice.

Meanwhile, says the Holy Father, you may be unwanted in the industrial world, but God has a job waiting for you. A greater, a higher, a more spiritual work than any other work. To be a spiritual producer, harvesting in your own soul a new abundance of the fruits of Redemption, and then to become a distributor likewise, an apostle bringing these fruits to others.

In this idea, too, that men must accept their new leisure and use it for noble ends, Pius XI has said a word that should not be soon forgotten.

October, 1933.

THE COMING LEISURE

HOW strange that any Catholic should be afraid of this leisured era which is now upon us. There is nothing particularly Catholic about the incessant drudgery that has marked modern industrialism. In the Catholic middle ages they understood well enough that man should work to live, not live to work. They believed strongly in holidays, and plenty of them.

'The Decretals of Gregory IX (about 1234) mention forty-five public feasts and holy days, which means eighty-five days when no work could be done. . . . From the thirteenth to the eighteenth centuries there were dioceses in which the holy days and Sundays amounted to over one hundred, not counting the feasts of particular monasteries and churches.' (*Catholic Encyclopedia* VI, 22.)

And that was in the ages of scarcity, of individual struggle against nature with bare hands and primitive tools. Holidays so numerous were often a genuine hardship to poor men. But the general conscience was determined to make time for the Mass and for all that social and educational and artistic side of life which centred round the Mass in those days. Even when the feast-days were cut down by Urban VIII, there still remained thirty-six, not counting Sundays.

That was in the year 1642, which in England saw the battle of Edgehill. Calvinism, Puritanism, and industrialism made short work of holy days and holiday-making. When there were no longer any rest-days in honour of God, it was considered a great boon when Lubbock managed to secure for Englishmen four holidays a year in honour of the Bank of England.

An English Bank Holiday at its best, or a fine month of August, gives some indication of what our nation could still do with holidays on the mediæval scale, especially if all workers were paid during holidays, as some are. The absence of money is rather a snag to any holiday.

All mankind now seems destined to become a leisured class. Unless we adopt the despairing policy of suppressing for mankind's good all machines and all scientific improvements in production (as some of the Nazis and some of our extreme Distributists seem to suggest) there will be less and less necessary work for men to do. Everybody will be more or less unemployed, and it will seem absurd to go on treating millions of men as an outcast and inferior race simply because they have found no employer.

True, the State could make employment for many by vast public works, with shorter hours and higher rates of wages, but as time went on there would be less and less left to be done ; and meanwhile there would still be a Poor-law class of blameless unemployables of one kind and another.

No ; the easiest way, the fairest way, and the best way of making the wheels of economic life go round, will be to give everybody an income—sufficient purchasing-power to provide a decent living—and make no conditions with it as to work. People will make their own work. Necessary drudgery might be left to those who would volunteer for it out of love for it or out of public spirit ; or it might be divided evenly all round in some scheme of compulsory service during youth ; or it might be competed for by those who wish to increase their income to buy luxuries and expensive holidays.

The point is to accept the age of leisure whole-heartedly, and break the connection between work and earning a living. To give to everyone, in fact, what the advocates of Social Credit call the National Dividend.

Many find this idea horrifying and dangerous. Is it not a return to the degenerate days of Imperial Rome, when the citizens were demoralised by free bread and free circuses ? *Panem et circenses !*

Well, bread is a good thing, and circuses are not so bad, though personally I don't like to watch performing animals. What was wrong with the Roman Empire was not the plentifulness of bread or the frequency of circuses, but rather the vast accumulations of capital, the institution of slavery, and the unrestricted operations of moneylenders ; all of which resulted in the free citizens losing their ownership and independence.

As to the moral effects of leisure on human nature, we are not after all left to mere speculation. In most countries there always has been a leisured class of people—a class with plenty of time on their hands and sufficient money to relieve them from anxiety about everyday needs. Such people have always had their own faults and temptations, just as the poor have too. But on the whole their leisure has not brought them to moral disaster.

Some of them have been idle and vicious, some of them merely ornamental, some of them have worked hard for the general good, or been leaders in artistic matters, or thinkers, or saints. What is true of the privileged classes of the past would be true of all other men and women if they had similar opportunities. There is nothing to be afraid of.

It seems likely that only the Church, in the long run, has sufficient command over the motivating forces of human life to produce a constant supply of men and women willing to work unselfishly for the happiness of their fellow-men. Consequently it will be once more the rôle of the Church, as in the Middle Ages, to teach men how to use their leisure, and how their holidays, just as much as their work, can be lived for God.

Already, as if by some divine instinct, the mind of the Church has been feeling its way in that direction. The movement for frequent and daily communion, for instance, is one which could never come to its full fruition under the pressure of industrial conditions of life. The liturgical movement, too, is gathering strength in preparation for the days to come when men will have time for God in their social life and when Christ shall be King indeed.

We are finding out how much time can be spent (and how joyously) over such a comparatively minor

E

matter as the Church's chant. New religious foundations such as the Grail, with freer organisation and more modern rules, are springing up all over the Church, to meet, in one way or another, this problem of education for leisure. The renascence of amateur religious drama is only one sign of something that is everywhere stirring in the Catholic mind and heart. The pilgrimage-habit is another ; and the cordial blessing which the Church gives to the Scout movement and to the modern interest in athletic sports— the list could easily be continued.

So why are you fearful, ye of little faith ? The earning of one's living is not an end in itself. Leisure is nothing to be afraid of, even if it is accompanied with an income.

Catholics need not prepare to creep away into the catacombs. They can go into the new epoch more confidently than anyone else, with their heads up and their eyes open ; and they will know how to act when they get there, at least the younger generation of Catholics will.

MONEY AND WAR

PEOPLE are once more talking of war as being near and inevitable, as in 1913. Many unimaginative people would welcome it. Some of the unemployed say ' Let's have another war.'

They know that war is the only way hitherto experienced of getting the bankers to create enough purchasing-power for everybody.

For so-called statesmen, in difficulties with unemployment, war is the easy line of least resistance. It gets the factories going, solves the problem of consumption.

As for the bankers themselves, they don't particularly like war, but they don't particularly object to it. War-time or peace-time, munitions or armaments, loans or reparations, inflation or deflation— they are going to gain either way.

Whether they understand what they are doing or not, it is the moneylenders of Threadneedle Street and Lombard Street, and their like in other countries, who bring about wars in the modern world.

They discovered long ago that what pays them best is to issue loans to foreigners abroad and to factories at home. The foreigners can only go on paying them interest by trading with the big countries where the moneylenders have their offices.

It suits the moneylenders therefore to keep the big countries dependent on foreign trade and foreign markets, and they can do this because the power of issuing credit puts the very soul of production (as the Pope says) into their grasp. Credit is available to make goods to sell abroad, but not for vital developments at home, such as the land.

Result : all the industrialised countries turning out manufactured goods at high pressure, shutting each other's goods out by tariffs walls, and struggling fiercely for the ever-dwindling markets provided by countries not yet industrialised. The end of economic war is military war.

Pope Pius XI traces the process by which ' those who can govern credit ' plunge the world into war :

' First there is the struggle for dictatorship in the economic sphere itself ; then the fierce battle to obtain control of the State, so that its resources and authority may be abused in the economic struggles ; finally, the clash between States themselves.'

Modern wars are fought to keep the factories going with markets and raw materials, so that the moneylenders may continue to receive the double flow of interest, from their factories at home and their foreign loans abroad.

In short, the financial system of the world is now such that it is bound to explode into war every few years.

Social credit is the only way to prevent the modern causes of war. Social credit would enable each country to issue enough purchasing power to its own inhabitants, and the resulting expansion of its home market would render unnecessary the international economic rivalry that leads straight to war. International trade would become a friendly exchange of goods not produced at home.

Meanwhile, the moneylenders know how to extract the last drop of profit out of the present fearful situation. Wars and even rumours of wars can be capitalised. In the next chapter let us look at the connection between the Banks and the armament firms.

September, 1933.

MONEY AND ARMAMENTS

THERE are many queer trades, but surely the queerest is the one which has for its direct material purpose the killing, maiming, disembowelling, blinding, poisoning, and choking of young men.

Though, perhaps, we ought to say women and children instead of young men, since Mr. Baldwin warns us that to save ourselves in the next war we shall have to 'kill more women and children more quickly than the enemy.'

I am not a pacifist. A just war of defence is not against God's Commandments, though I do not see how it can be reconciled with the Christian counsels (supposing any nation desired to live by them), unless in the case of attack by cruel and murderous invaders out simply to destroy. There is much to be put down on the credit side of war's balance-sheet. But that does not change the main fact, which is that modern scientific warfare has become, for mankind at large, a suicidal insanity.

'A bloody mug's game!' I heard a weary stretcher-bearer say, as he threw himself down for a few moments' rest about dusk on July 1, 1916. In the wide social sense his words were absolutely right. Another little war or two, with all the latest inventions of the slaughter-specialists, and our civilisation, with all its hopes and plans, will soon enough be one with Nineveh and Tyre.

Disarmament would not stop wars, though it would lessen their destructiveness at the beginning and give more chance to second thoughts. In any case, whatever arms a Government needs it can reasonably be left to manufacture for itself. As for the private-armament-industry, it is an international chain-store whose headquarters are in Hell.

The great combines—Vickers of Britain, Schneider-Creusot of France, Skoda of Czecho-Slovakia, Bethlehem Steel (what a name to choose !) of U.S.A., Mitsui of Japan, Krupp of Germany—are forging again those numerous links and inter-connections which in pre-war days made them and their predecessors into one great ring for the exploiting of men's worst passions.

It is the business of their inventors to think out ever more frightful and efficient engines of destruction, while their salesmen see to it that every country shall feel obliged to adopt them.

When the private armament trade was debated in Parliament (February 14, 1934) the War Office spokesmen defended its continuance by saying that its abolition would mean throwing large numbers of men out of work ; and then in the same breath he said it would mean that the Government would have to increase its own armament manufacture, wasting money on munitions that might never come into use. This is exactly the kind of insane reasoning that becomes necessary for those who defend the financial system. The private armament trade, in spite of all its dangers and objectionable features, must be kept on to provide employment and/or to save

money. Employment is set up as an end in itself,
yet it is reckoned extravagant to provide Government employment by making munitions that may
never be used. Evidently the only sound military
and financial solution is to keep our private armament firms going by making munitions for countries
which are foolish enough to use them, or perhaps
for our future enemies.

The armament firms claim to be doing a necessary
work of patriotism. But they supply all-comers,
including the likely enemies of their own country,
and to make sure of doing so they have their branches
and subsidiary companies in as many other countries
as possible.

Last year one English firm was advertising its
field-guns in a military journal in Germany. This
year another English firm announced a much-
improved type of armour-piercing shell which they
have patented in eight countries ; so that in the
next war our men will probably be killed by shells
actually being made in England now.

It is most notably in France that the armament
industry has bought over the newspapers and is able
to influence public opinion by scares and rumours of
war.

American armament-firms have admitted paying
25,000 dollars to an ' observer ' who did ' publicity
work ' for them at the Geneva Naval Conference in
1927 ; his efforts there seem to have been to prevent
arms-limitation, to spread anti-British propaganda,
to discredit peace-advocates, and so on.

To-day, then, as always, the armament industry

thrives on national suspicions and hatreds. It is like a huge malignant growth in the suffering body of humanity.

And now to the chief point. The armament industry, like any other industry, depends for its success and expansion upon the favour of ' those who are able to control credit and determine its allotment.'

Banks and bankers probably have direct holdings in armament firms, though information about this is not available. But banks can be more useful to the armament industry in other ways, by providing the credit backing for its developments, and more especially by providing its customers, the Govern-ments, large and small, with loans to make their purchases. France especially has used this method of gaining power over the small countries : loans by French banks, guaranteed by the French Government, to buy French armaments.

On the boards of directors of Vickers and Vickers-Armstrong there are 15 directors who hold between them 127 directorships. The Bank of England is represented by one of its most important figures, who is connected with two other banks also. The chairman of Vickers is also chairman of the Anglo-International Bank and director or partner in the banking firm of Glyn, Mills and Co., in the Bank of Rumania, Ltd., and the London Committee of the Ottoman Bank, as well as in two great insurance companies. Another director is a member of four banks or investment companies, another of two, another of the Securities Management Trust, and so on.

Names and particulars will be found in a book recently published by Mr. Fenner Brockway, *The Bloody Traffic*, which also gives a long string of similar facts relating to banking connections of Schneider-Creusot.

If the power of credit-creation were taken out of private hands and operated by a decent Government, it could be used for the common good, to abolish the slums, and so on, instead of feeding this appalling cancer of the armament trade.

The ' few men ' who, according to the Pope, exercise an irresistible financial domination in the modern world are lunatics quite capable of destroying mankind in their blind greed of money and power, unless mankind can find some way of putting them under restraint.

MONEY AND CHRISTIAN CHARITY

CHARITY is the most beautiful word in the English language, and it is hateful to the ears of nearly every Englishman. This, too, is the doing of the money system. Charity needs a foundation of Justice. Where Justice lies murdered, the springs of Charity are poisoned.

For the first sixteen centuries of the Christian Church, charity had a full social significance. It was the recognised way of effecting that redistribution of purchasing-power which everybody knew to be a continuous necessity.

From the first Pope onwards, every Bishop and theologian transmitted the same undiluted teaching : that God made the earth for all men ; that the owner of wealth is but a trustee for God ; that ownership of land or goods may be private but the use of them is common to all ; that all goods beyond the owner's needs should be given to the poor ; that all men have a right to the necessaries of life ; and that Jesus Christ will judge us according to how we treat His brethren the poor. To give away one's superfluity was an obligation and only the alms of profiteers and usurers were refused. The connection of Justice with Charity was complete, like the union of soul with body.

When the parochial system of Charity broke down

in the turmoils of the Dark Ages, the feudal lords, the guilds, the municipalities, and, above all, the monasteries took up the burden with undiminished sense of responsibility.   After thirteen hundred years St Thomas Aquinas states the social obligations of Charity as uncompromisingly as ever, and quotes with approval St Ambrose as saying that ' whatever a man keeps beyond his own needs is kept by violence.'   The goods of the Church in particular were ' the patrimony of the poor.'   Many a Bishop in the olden days, when some mediæval equivalent of the Means Test was driving men to despair, sold the cathedral treasures merely as a gesture of sympathy to keep a few hundred poor people in food for a few days or weeks longer.

So much for the Middle Ages.   Their teaching was clear, even if they did not always live up to it. And then,—the gold ships from America, and the moneylenders with their innocent-looking bits of paper, and John Calvin to tell them it was quite all right.   More scholarship than mine would be needed to trace what happened to the idea of charity amid the crash of the age-long Catholic teaching on the nature of money and the obligations of wealth. The theologians were asserting the duty of the Christian state to take care of the needy and unfortunate, but something had happened to the very notion of Christian brotherhood and solidarity itself. Money had become an instrument—*the* instrument —of power, and none of it seemed superfluous. Those who had it wanted to accumulate more and more of it, certainly not to give it away.   It was easy to argue ' Am I my brother's keeper ? ' easy to talk about ' the evil of begging ' and the need of making Poor Laws properly deterrent.

St Vincent de Paul was perhaps the last Catholic to conceive of charity as a permanent campaign of social justice, a continual redistribution of purchasing power ; but already the old imperious tone is gone. With St Vincent, the Church is frankly begging from the rich, persuasively no doubt, but begging, not commanding.

When we come to Ozanam—bright star in a dark hour—there is nothing left of the ancient alliance between charity and justice. Social Justice is despaired of, left for dead to anybody who cared to try artificial respiration (to a certain bushy-bearded Jew deep in books at the British Museum, for instance) and the devotees of charity must be content with relieving the little they can relieve of the misery around, partly to sanctify their own souls, partly to avert red revolution, but definitely not to remodel the economic order or make it more to God's desire.

Ambulance work, well organised, efficient, much needed, but ambulance work behind the battle— that is what the glorious and terrible Queen of the Virtues has come down to in our days.

That is at its best. At its worst—well, you have that appalling English phrase ' cold as charity.' The Money Power always seeks to keep money scarce, always likes to have a waiting queue of wage-slaves kept submissive by hunger. So Charity under the Money Power is always in dread of being too generous. It resents being taxed by the State for the poor, and is always seeking to cut down the ' social services.' It talks much of the ' undeserving poor,' is much given to paid officials and suspicious investigations, it gives tickets for groceries lest its money should be misused, stamps its mark on the boots lest they should be pawned. So the poor learn to hate and despite charity, even while they scramble for it, and some of them would rather die than touch it.

Nothing can take the place of justice. It may seem extravagant to say that there is more injustice to the poor now than ever before, but it is true, because for the first time in history there is plenty available for them, and it is being destroyed in front of their eyes to suit the schemes of a few money-lenders. As for charity, private charity is precious as always, but its alms-giving has little or no social significance. Public charity fails, because it makes terms with injustice and still lives mentally in the past ages of scarcity. The real work of charity to-day, the all-inclusive corporal Work of Mercy, the supreme demand of our Lord Jesus Christ from the present generation, is to bring our cruel and insane money system into correspondence with the needs of suffering mankind.

MONEY AND MARRIAGE

' I OFTEN wonder what God thinks of the scribes
and orators who thunder terrors at poor women
for their desperate attempts at contraception, and
yet have never a word to say to the Bank of England
and the Treasury, which have so obviously chosen
birth-restriction as the solution for unemployment
and are enforcing this policy on the poor by every
means in their power.'

So writes a man I know, and the only reply I can
think of is that I wonder too. Indeed our domination by the moneylenders is nowhere so disastrous
as in the sphere of marriage and family life.

For bringing up a family the first requisite is
evidently an income. Under the savage economies
of the past two years the children of the unemployed
have been allowed 2s. a week, and this morning's
paper (February 21, 1934) states that the Government, in face of entreaties from members of every
party, has refused to put a minimum of 3s. into the
new Unemployment Bill. 'Leave it to the Public
Assistance Board,' says the Minister of Labour,
'and perhaps they will give even more than 3s.'
The same paper says that the Government does not
expect the new Bill to be in operation before the
autumn, so the children's chances are rather remote
anyhow. But in such Government hopes and

promises there is always the implied condition ' if
the conditions of sound finance permit.'   Moneylenders will come first, the welfare of the children
second.

The right to marry is a primary human right like
the right to breathe and eat and the right to own
some property. Equally fundamental is the right
to bring up a family. The family is the basic social
unit, ordained as such by God Himself. Economic
systems must be arranged to suit the family, not the
family to suit economic systems. When Leo XIII
demanded the living wage, it was a family living wage
that he meant. All this is ordinary Catholic teaching.

Some time ago the papers mentioned that over
a certain period 236 young men, in Newcastle
I think, had got married ' on the dole,' and many
indignant ratepayers no doubt thought it was a great
scandal that such a thing should be allowed. An
ecclesiastical moralist, in fact (who is otherwise a
good sort and will not mind my quoting him), told
me he considered that a man should not marry until
he can undertake to support his wife and family
himself. That sounds reasonable enough and so it
might be in any ordinary period of the world's
history. It simply means having a reasonably
safe job or function in life, and being willing to work.
But where are the safe jobs nowadays, and how far
does willingness to work take you ?

Presumably, just as a whole generation of young
men had to be shot down in the mud and wire to
enable English generals to learn their job, so the new
generation of young men must make up their minds

to lifelong celibacy, so that all the Cabinet Ministers and suchlike may have ample time to readjust their ideas of economics. That is what it comes to.

I confess my sympathies were with the 236 young men. No doubt they thought that if they waited for things to improve, they would be as likely to wait fifty years as five. And one may fairly ask, what sort of a country is this where in one town alone hundreds of boys are leaving school and growing up to full manhood without ever having had an opportunity to make a foothold for themselves in the social structure, or to be able to foresee any future for themselves beyond the next visit to the Labour Exchange or the next casual few weeks' work ? And what sort of laws are these laws of England that result in such wholesale disaster to human lives ?

When the unemployed are forbidden to marry without the permission of the Court of Referees, or the Minister of Labour, we shall know that we have crossed the final border-line into the Servile State, and are back in the days of Imperial Rome or of Uncle Tom's Cabin.

Even for those with a steady job, who can see some sort of future ahead, even for these love and marriage are rendered almost impossible by the financial system and its merciless device, the family Means Test. A lad who has to throw every penny of his small wage into the family food-fund in order to keep his still-young father and his brothers and sisters who are unemployed or still at school—what chance has he got to save up for marriage, or take his girl to the pictures, or even buy himself a decent suit of clothes to go a walk in ?

To a young man and woman who are hindered from marriage by circumstances or unjust regulations, or pressure of social opinion, there always lies open an infallible way of making the world change its tune. On one condition everybody will hasten to facilitate their marriage instead of hindering it. No wonder if that condition is frequently fulfilled.

' Y' want to forget y'self for a bit an' try t'understand how t'young 'uns must feel about all these 'ere goin's on i' t'world to-day.' So says Mrs. Bull to Mrs. Hardcastle in Walter Greenwood's recent novel, *Love on the Dole*, which I take leave to recommend, not indeed to those who know all about the dole already, but to those who know of it only from hearsay and not as a possibility for themselves. It is a remarkable book, and I should say it will rank as a historical document. With less anger and more compassion it would have been as great a book as Hans Fallada's *Little Man What Now*, that final picture of pre-Nazi Germany, with its memorable Bunny.

MONEY AND EDUCATION

THIS money-muddle affects everything, and nothing more than education. As long as money remains a private monopoly, as long as Governments go on borrowing instead of creating the money they need, so long will Governments be ' short of money ' even for the most necessary things that everybody wants done. And when politicians are cutting down expenditure, the very first thing they always think of to economise on is education.

Of course in a sane financial system education would be recognised as one of the best ways by which the authorities could stimulate employment and increase purchasing power. A hundred new schools would mean work for all building trades ; a thousand extra teachers would mean so many more consumers of food and clothing to make the agriculturist rejoice.

Any Government that understood its duty to the children of England would not only clear away the slums in five years (a thing which could be done easily enough, though not by the hidebound finance of men like Mr. Neville Chamberlain) but would also spend many millions of pounds on more teachers and school buildings and playgrounds and holiday camps and generous grants to every voluntary effort of such kind. Communist and Fascist Governments are not failing to appreciate and also exploit the discovery (made first by the English but never really used) that children and adolescents have and ought to have a group-life of their own, secular as well as religious, which can only flower into existence if the adult community makes it possible. More money, then, not less, is needed for education, and it is no use making any plans unless we are prepared to get the money obstacle out of the way first. At present every step depends on whether the nation has the ' money ' for it.

The moneylenders are not thinking about increasing employment or national welfare, still less about the health and happiness of children. They are thinking only of money and how they can make it breed more. Schools do not serve their purpose. Education can never ' pay,' and they will not allow the Government to spend much money on it. Hence the continual cheese-paring economies— buildings and equipment, salary-cuts, fewer teachers, more work for them, larger classes. The black shadow of the Treasury and the Bank of England creeps over the classrooms. This will happen repeatedly, every time there is ' financial stringency,' that is to say, whenever the banking system for its own purpose cuts off for a time the nation's money supply.

In Russia, which (strange as it may sound) is the only country where the internal financial system seems to fit in more or less with traditional Catholic teaching,* there seems to be plenty of money for

* See p. 19.

education. The amount set aside for education by the Soviet Budget of 1932 was 1,403 million roubles, which compares favourably with the 1,278 million roubles for Army and Navy. If the Budgets of the separate republics and localities are included, Russia's annual expenditure on education is about 5,000 million roubles.

Catholic educational grievances in this country all arise from the fact that the nation has no money to spare for education. Catholics are criticising the Hadow reorganisation scheme, which was welcomed by several of our bishops when it was first announced. The main idea of it—that schooling should take an entirely new turn after the age of eleven—is absolutely sound and necessary, and only ignorance can object to it. Unfortunately when the idea gets down to the ordinary administrators there is never enough money to do it properly. For reasons of economy they are driven to adopt a policy of large senior schools, with consequent refusal of approbation to smaller senior schools and new all-age schools. This policy, which fits in so awkwardly with Catholic parochial custom, has no essential connection with Hadow reorganisation. It is also for various reasons inconvenient to children, to parents, and to teachers. It is being adopted almost entirely on the grounds of economy. Catholic spokesmen therefore ought to attack not the Hadow scheme or the Board of Education but the Treasury and the Bank of England and the financial system which provides unlimited ' money ' for the armament firms but as little as possible for the children.

Every teacher ought to detest the rule of the moneylenders under which we now live, because every day he has to watch his devoted efforts being hindered and frustrated by this devil Mammon. Some teachers give their whole life to children drowning in the sea of poverty, holding them up during a few short school years, long enough to discover the beautiful possibilities in them, only to see them sink back, one school-generation after another, into the hopeless morass of slum homes and casual employment. Only teachers know (when they haven't become too hardened to notice) the consequences of poverty and the Means Test in terms of child life. For 1932 the nation's Chief Medical Officer reports forty thousand cases of malnutrition amongst children of school age. ' Malnutrition ' is a fairly advanced stage of starvation ; by the time its symptoms reveal themselves, irreparable damage has already been done, the doctors say. For every such case there must be a dozen other cases in earlier stages of ill-nourishment. Nothing else can be expected as long as ' sound finance ' allows only two shillings a week to feed and clothe the children of the unemployed, while everyone admits that even five shillings would not be enough for the strictest minimum diet, let alone clothing.

We must always bear in mind that there is no scarcity of things like food and clothing. There used to be, even in our own lifetime, but that is so no longer. Whatever scarcity there is now is an artificial scarcity caused by destroying things (wheat, for instance), or preventing their production, so as to make human life fit in with the existing money-system. It is difficult to believe that men behave so insanely, but the fact is so.

Intelligent teachers are numerous and they have a right to be heard on these topics. The work in which they share—the upbringing, physical, mental, and moral, of the recently-arrived members of the human race—is incomparably the greatest work of all. It is always the first thing to suffer at present, whenever the economy cry is raised, and it will be the very first thing to benefit when the Money Muddle is cleared up, which ought not to be very long now if the English character still has or can regain its capacity for action.

January, 1934.

MONEY AND ART

THERE is an inevitable connection between money and art, just as there is between money and religion ; and the connection does not always work out fortunately.

They say that Mr. Montagu Norman has a pretty taste in antiques, or old masters or whatever it is, and rumours of striking and original sculpture on the Bank's new buildings have reached even my Philistine ears. That may be so. Nevertheless in its relation to culture in general the English banking system is more stupid and boorish than the ox that sets his uncaring hoof on the first cluster of primroses. If there are too many cinemas and not enough schools, if living musicians starve and tinned music assails the tortured ear, if villages of bungalows are built on the skyline of the downs, and the English countryside is laid waste by ruthless industrialism—where is the ultimate blame if not on the credit-system which ' finds the money ' for such developments and insists on ' getting it back ' ?

Yet, strange to say, there are artists who look forward without enthusiasm to the reform of finance. Take, for instance, Mr. Eric Gill, who has lately written much on the topic, especially in his book, *Beauty looks after Herself*. Mr. Eric Gill, being an intelligent and humane person, perceives the insanity

74

of the present money-system and takes for granted that it will soon be changed. But in this prospect he sees no hope for the true artist. For him, the true artist means the perfect workman doing necessary work ; the age of plenty means the triumph of the machine and the extinction of responsible craftsmanship ; the age of leisure means a populace machine-fed, machine-clothed, with minds standardised and mass-produced opinions, spending their time in travel, sport, and the more frivolous kinds of ' love '-making, while art dwindles to a mere matter of water-colour painting and fancy-work. ' God save us,' says Mr. Eric Gill piously, ' from all the arts and crafts which are the product of leisure.'

On the other hand, there is Mr. Will Dyson, cartoonist and author of *Artist among the Bankers*. He sees modern life as a gigantic confusion of frustration and tyranny, with the stupid and obsolete money-system as the villain of the piece. Unemployment to him is the workman not being allowed to use his tools, being forbidden by Finance.

As for the modern art and literature, Dyson scorns them for occupying themselves with unreal trivialities, escaping from life rather than facing it. Even the supposed virtues of our literature, such as Humour, come under his condemnation. ' Humour and good humour are virtues in the private sphere, but elsewhere they are a cowardice and a thinness of the blood. . . . The world is too huge a joke to be laughed off. Laughter has lost its virtue, it is not a cure to-day, it is the neurosis itself.' Something personal in this remark may be guessed at by those

F *

whose memories go back far enough to compare Dyson's good-humoured drawings of to-day with the blistering ferocity of his pre-War cartoons, say at the time of the Dublin transport strike.

Business men, the so-called Practical men, having now made a complete muddle of human life, Dyson thinks it is time the Artist began to sit up and do something about it. An epochal fight is on, and the artist cannot stay out of it and keep his soul intact.

' Artists,' says Dyson, ' are the stewards of a thing higher than themselves—the art element in man— almost the religious element.' They know in their hearts that the Business Machine is a monstrous tyranny, and they must not fear to say so. ' It is time the Art Element took the offensive. . . . There is no other preoccupation for leisured men but the art habits. These are the activities of leisure. The art of the world is the product of the leisure of the world—of time snatched from the toil of the world—the toil dedicated to the needs of the belly and the back.'

I think Mr. Dyson is right, also that he and Mr. Eric Gill are in fundamental agreement. Nobody really wants to abolish work, and nobody could. How many men, for instance, can resist the urge to work if they have a house and garden of their own ? We should distinguish carefully between work and drudgery, defining drudgery as work which one is compelled to do without being somehow interested in it. The nearer we can come to abolishing drudgery the better ; and this does not necessarily mean abolishing digging or even machine-tending, both of which can be undertaken with interest by some people.

Perhaps the new Economics in the early stages of its preaching has received a slightly too mechanical bent owing to the fact that Major Douglas is an Engineer. To those who share the fears of Mr. Eric Gill, may I commend the following from a letter by John Rimmer in *New Britain* :

' There is an assumption that financial reform will achieve the mass consumption of mass production. But what if it destroys mass production ? . . . Terrifying statistics are given of the potentialities of the machine. Mr. Kenrick informs us that England can make two and a quarter pairs of boots or shoes for every inhabitant of the globe. But what happens if we distribute increased incomes on the strength of this and similar potentialities ? To date, machinery applied to boots and shoes has meant mainly the mass production of corns and bunions. We have put up with the wholesale crippling for reasons of the economy enforced upon us by non-co-operating finance, but increase our incomes sufficiently and we will insist on respect for pedegraphic peculiarities and order our hand-made pair. So with our clothing. At £2 per week we wear ready-mades. At £5 we are beginning to employ the cutter and hand-finisher. Thus labour saved at one end of the process of production is balanced at the other end for the ensuring of a more individualised product. Every man aches for the full expression of his individuality, and individualised consumption can only mean individualised production.

Ask the women if any machine-made jumper compares with the product of a skilled hand-knitter.

' This principle applies to all branches of production. For food, increased income means a demand for pedigree fruits and cereals and thus the revival of agricultural art and the personal attention of the gardener instead of agricultural industrialisation. For the building of houses the architect and building craftsmen come into the picture once more and the jerry builder exits. And so it is with the services. The present compulsory mass production in education will give way to a vast number of private schools and even individual tutelage ; wholesale medical treatment in the hospitals will yield to a great increase of private doctors and nurses. All this resulting from the consumer, allowed an increased income by the financial reform, more freely expressing his individual choice when making his purchases.

' So, in *New Britain*, I prophesy that the artist-craftsman will revive after his temporary eclipse, and the engineers will be—not quite so important.'

IN A NUTSHELL

CREDIT reform may never come about—there may not be enough collective intelligence and will in the world to bring it about. That remains to be seen. But conceivably it might come about quite soon in our own country or in Ireland. If it does come, it will make as much difference to man-kind as the invention of writing, or the mariner's compass, or motor-engines. As much difference in some ways and as little difference in others.

There has always been money and there have often been moneylenders, but during the last two hundred years the English bankers have built up a far more highly-developed money system than was ever seen before, and have taught the rest of the world to use it. First, gold became a universally accepted standard, and on that basis was built up a cheque system which enabled the banks to practise the art of money-lending with much greater freedom and with a minimum of actual cash. They found by experience that they could safely lend out much more ' money ' than they really possessed and get interest on it, too. On this financial foundation our great industrial system grew up and flourished.

When the War came, it enormously accelerated this development in two ways. First, all countries made great strides in machine-production ; after the War it soon became evident that not only shells and guns, but also food, clothing, and shelter could be produced in unprecedented plenty and that poverty could be easily abolished.   Secondly, the War loans were used by the banks as opportunities for creating credit on a gigantic scale, with a correspondingly gigantic burden of interest on the State to be raised by taxation.

The process has now reached a climax of absurdity. Millions are workless with work all round needing to be done, and millions are more or less starving in a world where food is so plentiful that it has to be destroyed.   All this simply because money does not circulate.   Because neither public authorities nor private employers can have money for wages or doles or any other purpose except by getting into debt to banks.

Credit reformers say that all this could be avoided if the King's Government kept in its own control the power of issuing money and credit, instead of letting the banks control it.

The movement towards a just Credit system has been growing along with the development of the banking system itself.   Gesell in Germany was thinking and writing about it in the 'nineties, and the Catholic school of Fribourg even earlier than that ; others like Eisler in Austria and Kitson in England were at it in pre-War days ; Major Douglas published his *Economic Democracy* in 1919, and since then new names like Professor Büchi (Germany) and Professor Soddy (England) have been numerous enough.

There is already quite a vast literature.   For the

ordinary general reader the readable, up-to-date book is *This Age of Plenty*, by C. M. Hattersley (Sir Isaac Pitman and Sons, 3s. 6d.). It is Douglasite but explains other shades of opinion also ; make sure you get the third edition, 1932. Cheap pamphlets are numerous. A good one called *Men and Money* is published at twopence by the Co-operative Union, Holyoak House, Hanover-street, Manchester.*

How does Credit Reform square with Catholic social teaching ? Very well indeed. Its analysis of present conditions is the same as the Papal criticisms of high finance in *Quadragesimo Anno* and *Caritate Christi compulsi*. Its positive proposals may be regarded as a modernised version of the Catholic doctrine of a Living Wage : give people enough money to buy the goods they collectively produce—that is what Social Credit comes to. In an age of plenty it becomes a matter of *justice* to ensure that everyone has enough.

How would a regime of socialised credit affect the prospects of the Church ? Very favourably, one would imagine. Every cause that depended on people's free-will offerings would be in a better position. No more grinding poverty to keep people away from church. Churches and schools would go up as easily as bank-buildings and public-houses go up at present. With the fear of personal insecurity banished, avarice would tend to disappear, to the

* See also *The Breakdown of Money*, by C. Hollis (Sheed & Ward 4/6), and *Promise to Pay*, by Dr. McNair Wilson (Routledge 3/6).

great advantage of the Church of God. With more travel, Catholics would appreciate more the catholicity of the Church. The liturgy could come into its own—parochial sung Mass every day—(even now the unemployed have the leisure for it, but who has the heart?).

To the Church will fall the colossal but inspiring task of showing men how to use their free time worthily. Education will become the all-absorbing interest of the most devoted minds—education itself, not the mere administration of it. The Church will once more summon her handmaidens, music, drama, the arts and the handicrafts—to help her teach men the art of living and the kind of work that is worth doing. New forms of charity will be needed, new religious orders. . . .

Well, that is looking ahead. An age of leisure is quite certain indeed. This is already an age of leisure for millions and millions. But they are not enjoying it. Perhaps we shall go on just as we are, with millions of unemployed leading a dismal existence and slowly dwindling in numbers by enforced birth control. But it is more than possible that there is enough intelligence and will in England to assert itself, convince the so-called ' practical ' people, or push them aside if necessary, and make the needed adjustments in our economic life before breakdown and decay have gone too far.

THE OPPORTUNITY OF ENGLAND

SOME people think I ought not to write so vindictively (as they consider) about members of the Government. My only defence is that on one thing, at all events, I agree with the Hitlers and Stalins and Mussolinis—namely, on the doctrine of *responsibility*, and the need of fixing it.

However, for a change, let us praise at least one member of the Government. Except for a tendency (probably not of his own choosing) to the destruction and limitation of food-output in England, a tribute of respectful admiration can safely be offered to Mr. Walter Elliot, the Minister of Agriculture. His actions are almost Rooseveltian for vigour, and when he speaks he has something to say. Listen to this :

' The country is, as sound as a bell,' says Mr. Walter Elliot. ' We want to have a revolution in this country, but a revolution of progress. We want to do it better than anybody else, and above all, we want to see it orderly and without the accompaniment of riots and bloodshed in the streets.' Now that's the way to talk, isn't it ? If only some of the others—well, never mind !

It is true that England ought to be able to do it better than anybody else. Partly because having watched the revolutionary experiments of the others, we should be able to learn from their mistakes, and partly because we have plenty of our own mistakes to learn from. The money power arose first in England, and how fitting it would be if England were the first country to dethrone it successfully, and show the world how to combine planned economy with individual freedom. The intellectual part of this work has already been mostly done, and Englishmen with Scotsmen of course ! have done it.

Amongst all the proposed remedies for our troubles, Social Credit—by which I mean the establishing of any sane money-system that would correspond to the real facts of human life and production—is the remedy that is central. That is to say, it includes or implies all the ' isms,' all the good points of the other proposed remedies. Communism and Fascism especially, the only two alternatives as they seem to many,· would both be rendered unnecessary in any country which would begin by remodelling its money-system by the light of Catholic ideals.

Being truly central and inclusive, Social Credit is naturally unpopular with all the sections whose vision is fixed on some particular side of the problem. Socialism and Distributism, for instance, wide apart as they are, both agree in saying that money reform does not go to the root of anything. The banking system, they say, is no more to blame than the big industrial combines with which it is mingled so inextricably. No use reforming money unless you also reform the ownership of property. Socialists want State ownership, Distributists want peasant proprietorship and small businesses ; both of them agree in regarding ownership—the acquisitive instinct of man—as the all-important factor.

Is not this psychology a survival from the age of scarcity ? Men wanted to claim land and material possessions as their very own, they hoarded up quantities of food and furniture and clothing and gold, because they feared scarcity. But nobody wants to do that in the age of plenty, and we are all rapidly ceasing to honour people according to their accumulation of material possessions. Even the old virtues of thrift and saving are under serious suspicion nowadays.

Very little children often cry if somebody else plays with their toys ; but except for infants and infantile minds there is no longer any magic in *mere* ownership of material things. There is magic in property in the true sense, in having what is *proper* to one's nature and state; magic in responsibility, in control, in security of tenure, yes—but that is different.

Ownership of land and material goods was sought because it was a title to economic security joined with freedom. Perhaps it still is to some extent, but dubiously. Every owner knows that however well he manages, the moneylender is waiting for him and may get him in the end. If it is a case of economic security and freedom, most people would feel safer with a balance at the bank, or an unearned income of some kind.

When there are plenty of things to buy, money is more useful than property. As the age of plenty arrives, the whole Socialist controversy about private ownership becomes unreal and obsolete, and the old Catholic doctrines re-emerge as fresh as paint—the right of individual ownership in material things, the right of the community to share the use of them, and—always in reserve for any emergency—the *altum dominium* of the civil authority.

At the same time there is a return to another set of Catholic ideas—the grouping of free men into responsible guilds, leading naturally to a self-governing Assembly for the nation's economic affairs.

For all these objectives, Social Credit (in the broad sense already explained) will be found to provide the only method of orderly and peaceful attainment. Other ways perhaps lie open to the promised land of economic security, but no other way that is compatible with the English ideal of individual freedom.

January, 1934.

THE END

The Mayflower Press, Plymouth   William Brendon & Son, Ltd

www.ingramcontent.com/pod-product-compliance
Lightning Source LLC
La Vergne TN
LVHW091205080426
835509LV00006B/838